THE DROID

BY CHRISTINA EARLEY

ILLUSTRATED BY

ANASTASIA KLECKNER

A Blue Marlin Book

SEAHORSE
PUBLISHING

Introduction:

Phonics is the relationship between letters and sounds. It is the foundation for reading words, or decoding. A phonogram is a letter or group of letters that represents a sound. Students who practice phonics and sight words become fluent word readers. Having word fluency allows students to build their comprehension skills and become skilled and confident readers.

Activities:

BEFORE READING

Use your finger to underline the key phonogram in each word in the *Words to Read* list on page 3. Then, read the word. For longer words, look for ways to break the word into smaller parts (double letters, word I know, ending, etc.).

DURING READING

Use sticky notes to annotate for understanding. Write questions, make connections, summarize each page after it is read, or draw an emoji that describes how you felt about different parts.

AFTER READING

Share and discuss your sticky notes with an adult or peer who also read the story.

Words to Read:

boip	toib	factoids
coils	voice	jetfoil
doin	boing	noises
hoin	droid	oily
loip	joints	ointment
noid	oink	poison
Oi	point	rejoice
roid	android	turquoise
soib	avoid	hydrofoils

4

"Oink! Boing! Oink! Boing!"

The android is only making funny noises. What is it trying to say?

It might need some oily ointment in its coils and joints.

That worked! It can talk now!

"Boip! Loip! Boip! Loip!

My name is Oi. I am a droid. I use my voice to give factoids."

Great
South Bay

"Noid! Roid! Noid! Roid!

A Blue Point oyster is
an oyster that has lived at
least three months in Great
South Bay, New York."

"Hoin! Doin! Hoin! Doin!

Beware the poison dart frog. The bright turquoise skin emits poison. Avoid this animal!"

"Toib! Soib! Toib! Soib!

A jetfoil is a boat that flies on top of water. It uses wings called hydrofoils. Rejoice that it uses less fuel."

Quiz:

1. **True or false?** A dart frog's skin has poison.
2. **True or false?** A jetfoil is a type of car.
3. **True or false?** A Blue Point oyster must live for three months in Great South Bay.
4. What did the droid need at the beginning of the story? How do you know?
5. Why do you think a dart frog's skin is poisonous?

Flip the book around for answers!

Activities:

1. Write a story in which at least one character is a droid. What special features does the droid have?

2. Write a new story using some or all of the "oi" words from this book.

3. Make a song to help others learn the sound of "oi."

4. Sort the "oi" words from this book into categories. What do the words in each category have in common?

5. Create a meme about the "oi" key word "droid."

Written by: Christina Earley
Illustrated by: Anastasia Kleckner
Design by: Rhea Magaro-Wallace
Editor: Kim Thompson
Educational Consultant: Marie Lemke, M.Ed.
Series Development: James Earley

Library of Congress PCN Data
The Droid (oi) / Christina Earley
Blue Marlin Readers
ISBN 979-8-8873-5293-0 (hard cover)
ISBN 979-8-8873-5378-4 (paperback)
ISBN 979-8-8873-5463-7 (EPUB)
ISBN 979-8-8873-5548-1 (eBook)
Library of Congress Control Number: 2022951099

Printed in the United States of America.

Seahorse Publishing Company

seahorsepub.com

Published in the United States
Seahorse Publishing
PO Box 771325
Coral Springs, FL 33077